Let yourself feel each colour at a time, breathe in
and out slowly. We can feel too much at once,
sometimes nothing at all. Even when we see red,
or feel blue, we need to remember that the sun
shines orange, even when we don't feel her
warmth. The trees show us every version of
themselves, when stripped bare, when burnt
yellow, or the deepest green. We appreciate the
journey, we welcome the growth. Let's show
ourselves the same love.

Contents

5. Silver Lining
6. So Many Left To Love
7. Feeling Blue
8. Beneath My Feet
9. Sound To Story
10. Pink To Make Myself Wink
11. If The Shoe Was On The Other Foot
13. A Seed Of Doubt
14. The View
15. A Sisters Promise
16. Paint The Town Red
17. Ode To Bristol
18. 50 Lovers Lane
19. Something At The Door
20. Good As Gold
21. Ageing Like Champagne
22. Day 2 Day
23. Once In A Blue Moon
24. One Step Closer
25. A Solo Adventure
26. Reflection
27. A Bad Hand
28. Sinking
29. Olive Tree
30. A Glass Of Orange Juice
31. Lost In The Wind
32. Pink Lady
33. Not Your Home
34. To Be Found
35. The Tea Tree
36. White Flag
37. Forever In The Sycamore
38. Strawberry Summer
39. Into The Flames

40. Empty Vase
41. Don't Be Scared Of The Spider
42. Silent Lovers
43. Home Bird
44. Colours That Make Me Feel Safe
45. Soul Searching
46. Intimacy
47. Tainted Waters
48. Feel Like Summer
49. Passing Pictures
50. Grief In Life
51. Waking At Sunset
52. Moving Time
53. Sea Of Green
54. Something In The Water
55. Comfort Blanket
56. Head 2 Head
57. Grey Area
58. Mother's Love
59. Simplicity
60. To The Core
61. Sun Birth
62. Aries Moon
63. Your Garden
64. Whole
65. Love Like Them
66. Flying Colours
67. Leaving Me
68. Finding Her
69. Colours That Make Me Feel Alive
70. I Want To Feel
71. Growing And Glowing
72. The Way It Goes

Silver Lining

I tried to find the silver lining
I even drew it on the page
but even when silver is shining
it can sometimes be confused with grey

When I drew it on the page
the line could not be seen
I tried so hard to gauge
where the line had been

To find a silver lining is misleading
as hope isn't linear
we lose it as much as we gain it, through healing
often to it we feel inferior

In order to find my silver lining
I need to go on my silver journey
a turbulent voyage, all defining
where finally I'll be worthy

So Many Left To Love

Too much space taken up in my mind
for people I have lost on my journey
mourning friendships that didn't survive
old lovers who ended up not worthy

When I think it's run its course
I've met everyone I'm ever going to love
this ideology I always reinforce
loving people I can't let go of

All the people I haven't met yet
I might love even more
I sometimes even bet
they'll be better than before

My first baby
a love I can't imagine
but maybe they'll save me
take my compassion

New friends I will meet along the way
love moving through waves
as life flows day by day
it will be their love that I save

Strangers I meet in places I pass
a moment in time kind of love
singing together at a concert on the green grass
those moments are always enough

So much time, to meet so many people
I know I won't ever regret
so when I feel alone, the next part of the sequel
getting ready to love people I don't know yet

Feeling Blue

I can't stop feeling blue
I needed to colour match my skin
they told me "I know we're B&Q
but I think you need to look within"

I spent all night painting myself orange
hoping to cancel out the navy
I ate my morning porridge
then wondered what would save me

I consulted Pantone
to get myself diagnosed
I was sure I'd get Azure though
even Cyan they might propose

I went outside that day
a stranger said I reminded her of the sky
my head did feel cloudy - far away
but that comment got me by

Although I'm feeling blue
there is beauty in this colour
so instead I let the sun shine through
cleared the clouds, one after another

Beneath My Feet

He pulled the carpet from beneath my feet
the first one we ever purchased together
a Wednesday night trip to IKEA
fibres tangled with a lovers tale
to lay in our first home
number 11, Church Road

I wasn't religious but he was the highest entity
I worshipped the ground he paced
the one in which I found myself frozen
no carpet to console my fragile frame
he pulled the wool over my eyes
from the rug he picked, our first carpet

I couldn't see past what he painted
wool clung to my eyelashes like a fly to a web
a landscape, one solo house in a green meadow
situated above the old coal fire, the centrepiece
he used thread and dye to manipulate me
we were two very different artists

I used mine for good, he used his for gain
that for sale sign cut deep
more damage to my organs than to my skin
I didn't let him stay under it, even though he tried
I used the wool as a temporary nest
until my body was strong enough to be my new home

Sound To Story

Music spoke to me when I couldn't speak to myself
put my feelings into stories when life took the words
how beautiful to feel someone else's journey
for it to touch your soul with soft hands
for it to grab you like a lover
on a Saturday night booty call
or to move your body
a night spent with best friends
two strangers singing over a glass of red
connecting through intertwining thoughts
20,000 bodies screaming "you made me hate this city"
one line that makes us all feel lighter
now I hope you can feel my stories in your chest
burrowing deep inside your skin
setting some of your colours free
showing you colour that you've never seen

Pink To Make Myself Wink

I wore this colour for myself
I didn't need validation from anyone
I grabbed a book off the top shelf
decided to have a picnic in the sun

Took myself on a date
dressed as a strawberry milkshake
I felt like it was almost fate
as I tucked into my cheesecake

It's so important to treat yourself sometimes
especially wearing your favourite outfit
drinking lemonade with freshly cut lime
listening to music until the sky is moonlit

- date yourself

If The Shoe Was On The Other Foot

I was two feet tall and ready to take on the universe
dreams of being a leader is what I rehearsed
when I reached six feet, I realised it wasn't that easy
twenty people apply for one job, what would make them pick me?

Out of all these people, they only accept one
they say it's fair game but he was the CEO's son
he became the manager, I worked underneath him
how can we compete with what the companies are teaching?

He always looked strong and composed
his muscular build in his tight shirt was never too exposed
but my high heeled shoes were too seductive
I distracted the men from being productive

Maybe it was being taller that was too intimidating
he wanted to look down on me, when he couldn't it was frustrating
reminiscing on my youth flooded with ambition
being told what to wear was not part of this position

Payday came and then I was inclined
to buy the most expensive pair of high heels I could find
I went to work the following day
rushed to find the boss, as I had something to say

'You are familiar with designers, so you'll know these are
Jimmy Choo, they make me even taller, so now I'm
looking down on you. If my shoes make you lose
concentration, then today, I'm handing in my resignation"

It turns out my shoes were extremely rare
I sold them on and became a millionaire
I took over the company and got the boss fired
then made sure more women were hired

They all got high heels to wear with pride
just as a little message to say
by the rules we will abide
but only if the rules are equal on both sides

A Seed Of Doubt

He asked me for directions
I don't know if he knew I was the one that was lost
maybe he could see in my reflection
that to love, comes with a cost

How was he to know my baggage was full of seeds
I said I'd plant them without a doubt
but what I didn't foresee
would be a period of drought

I promised myself I'd plant them when the time was right
a five year old pledge diluted by worry
a feeling that time is limitless in this life
I was only nineteen then, never in a hurry

I just sat on the outskirts
neither too quiet nor having outbursts
I just sat comfy in the middle
writing and finishing my own riddles

I spent most of the time trying to find my way home
one which we could share together
I needed an extra room to store my baggage alone
somewhere my seeds could grow in all weather

I don't know if this home exists
and right now I am astray
maybe if this drought persists
I can plant my seeds another day

The View

I looked through my circle window
eye level to building tops
I noticed how the wind would blow
how it listened when the trees told it to stop

The blue was almost translucent
the sky wanted me to see further
even when there's no movement
the clouds dance when I'm the observer

So many stories in each building
lots of stairs, where are they leading
broken souls ready for gilding
lots of stories, floor to ceiling

In each window a different face
one thing connecting us together
we live separate, but share one space
our pane of glass, the dancing weather

A Sisters Promise

I asked my body what she needed, she told me that she wants to make her own decisions, so many things decided for a female. She wasn't ready for a baby and if there was an accident, she needed a way out. She mumbled she wasn't maternal under her breath, embarrassed of her choices. I loved her but she wanted more independence, I told her today was a sad day for women, they are taking our freedom right before our eyes. She asked me why females would do that to other females, but I told her it was men who made the decisions. We needed a moment. She said they impregnate us against our will and make us keep it. She is still learning.

Women are resilient, like many who stood before us, have fought for our cause, many will stand after us, and continue to shed blood. I touched my body gently, she needed reassurance, this is our first step in taking back control. They have declared a war on us, and I am ready to fight. I will take it back, if I am not here, I will leave it to my sisters, a legacy only we can carry. My inheritance will be power, many bloodlines later we will regain control. My will, a scripture which will be studied in years to come, I will make sure it can't be misinterpreted. 50 lines carved on black stone
- *our bodies, our choice.*

Paint The Town Red

My friends wanted to paint the town red
they urged me to get out of bed
my safe place, maybe a little too safe
I needed to feel a different space

I wore converse so I could dance my socks off
sang Fleetwood Mac until I needed to cough
Laryngitis from Landslide, I feel it all too well
smothered in Black Opium, my favourite smell

I wore my dungarees
I am ready to feel free
a paintbrush gripped tightly
between my teeth it might be

It is tonight we cut the rope from our hands
feel our feet wherever they land
take the clip from out our hair
sing until our lungs need air

Even Stevie said thunder only happens when it's raining
so I better get painting
before it washes all the red away
and back again appears the grey

Ode To Bristol

On the number 42 bus
the same route I always take
the same people, same faces
the sticky bus seats with fabric awfully printed
like a Wetherspoons carpet
a colourful headache, stitched with reminiscence
a man joined to my hip, when 50 more seats lay before him
his leg a little too close to mine
up to Park Street past College Green
students soaking up friendships
sharing pizza and pints on the grass
learning nothing but the importance of memories
past Pinkmans Bakery
the best toastie
a flawless cheese pull
I can wander to the Museum
soak in the culture
visit the past more than once
go outside and do the same
wonder if I will see the same faces forever
nostalgia follows me everywhere in Bristol
I crave to feel something different
but familiarity is captivating
it's hard to leave what you know so well

50 Lovers Lane

I always wanted a yellow front door
my sunshine sanctuary
where light seeps through crooked floors
behind it, we live as one
two young bodies figuring out how to love
measuring it only in the weight it holds
an ounce of doubt
wondering if this is what it should feel like
but a ton of lessons
we will learn either way

Something At The Door

I sat alone with my mind
one by one I let the thoughts in
I tried my hardest to unwind
as the chaos did begin

I told them to form an orderly queue
but they never do listen
if only I knew
how to stop this division

With my thoughts I must align
they hold no substance
we must intertwine
although I am reluctant

We are stronger together
they must learn to be patient
and I must learn never
with my thoughts, be complacent

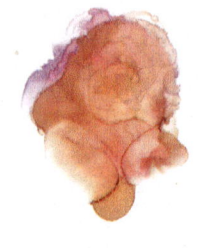

- if only they were this colourful

Good As Gold

I tried to be as good as gold
but isn't it refreshing to have a vice
something that doesn't keep you in a hold
leaves you feeling nice

Sometimes it's so tempting
to visit the old me
the girl that was preempting
who she could next be

One who was lost and confused
relied on being pretty
who felt like she was being used
for a ticket into the city

But oh did she feel attractive
she was confident and brave
always so proactive
in filling up her days

Instagram likes for affirmation
I don't need it anymore
but it did feel good to build a foundation
where I felt sexy and adored

She was my vice
I'm now good as gold
I think I'll visit her twice
anymore and she has her hold

Ageing Like Champagne

The grey roots spill out my skull like an overflowing bucket of threads
used to knit blankets covering cold limbs
now older, the warmth harder to keep
they said I've aged like fine wine
what they didn't see was how many grapes got stuck between these toes
how dancing with purple feet meant stained white carpets
ruined bed sheets
what if I want to age like champagne
gliding through rich lips, just one sophisticated evening
but each wrinkle a crater
I stick my fingers in to feel deeper, to touch memories
his hand on my thigh
before my skin reflected the damage of 20 suns
not even Aloe Vera offered me reassurance
fingers to tree bark
to count the circles in my stump
60 crooked rings holding 300 burnt leaves
if I scream in the woods and no one is there to hear me,
did I make a sound?
or have the years just taken my voice

Day 2 Day

I listened to brown noise
the most peace I've had all day

I swam in a cup of tea
a break from the disarray

The day wasn't busy
but my mind made jobs

Hung myself out to dry
after pairing my odd socks

I washed my hair 3 times
dried it with my grey rug

Hoovered up the tea
put away my mug

Once In A Blue Moon

I sat with my demon over a cup of coffee
I think it's about time I let her in
after years of wondering what she embodied
thinking who she could've been

I had visions in my head
of scary looking creatures
we both sat on my bed
whilst I admired her features

I hated my curly hair but it looked so good on her
I told her she must embrace it
but that conversation felt like a blur
as my own advice, I don't take it

She told me a problem shared is a problem halved
I asked her what she needed to tell me
she said to me over a bubble bath
it's only once in a blue moon that demons are scary

One Step Closer

What is your favourite colour?
A phrase that leaves lips like it's last months fashion trend
discarded so easily during opening conversations
I'd been asked too many times and I never know what to say
as my spirit is yellow but I see black more than anything
I want to normalise asking what you need from a relationship
what is your language of love?
words of affirmation
quality time
being held until you become sleepy
not because you're tired, but because you feel safe
not asking if I go to the gym
health isn't always fitness and a healthy relationship isn't always physical
take away the connotations from colour and they mean nothing
red is sexy
pink is feminine
yellow is bright
instead just ask me if I'm happy and I will tell you that
I am one step closer everyday

A Solo Adventure

I'm starting to realise
I'm worth more than I am getting
it seems so refreshing
to realise my worth
after years on this Earth
but late is better than never
just me and myself together
one pink flower on a solo adventure
flowers voluptuous, stalk slender

Reflection

When you sit back
think of how far you've come
it doesn't need to reflect
the numbers in a bank account
the four walls in which you reside
the wheel you sit behind
success is modest
it tiptoes through the darkness
sometimes disguised as
a brighter day
a kinder heart
a lesson learnt
softer words
clear boundaries
an even clearer mind
most importantly
a blooming garden
watered roots
vibrant flowers
a straight path
guided by sunlight

- sometimes the reflection is clearer after a storm

A Bad Hand

I kept my cards close to my chest
although I didn't like the hand I had been dealt
I still tried my best
to feel everything that needed to be felt

Always wanted Queen of Hearts
although I was bad at protecting mine
Ace of Spades is a good start
maybe it was a sign

I must not bury my troubles
easy as that may be
a spade can only dig so far into the rubble
past the roots of the brown oak tree

Sinking

I've sunk too far into the blue
not the lake I went swimming in that summer
floating in contentment, pure pleasure
not the melted bubblegum ice lolly staining my face and fingers
handprints on mums pink skirt
not a blanket of freesias hugging the park floor
I fell into as a child, running for the playground
I'm drowning in the blueberries I eat for breakfast
shoved in my ears telling me I must eat healthy
the bruises of twenty people who walked straight through me
an invisible sack of skin they pounded into to get to work
I never had anywhere to be
sinking into the gas fire
burning the wooden floor, covered with a blue sofa
I sink into it to write these poems
a blue point pen to transform my feelings into stories
each line I fall further, the profoundness turning me purple
recollecting fallen memories until my veins resemble worms in my head
wriggling until I set them free
through my fingers and onto this page

Olive Tree

We met under an olive tree
all that we knew was all that we could see
but I wanted more
so much left to be explored

It was the first taste of freedom
although I did need him
a bittersweet Sunday morning
the bright light dawning

By the end of the day I wouldn't be here
I might visit again next year
I needed something more
to see behind that door

The waves were waiting for me
I heard under the shade of the tree
them call my name, so vividly
to invite me deep into the sea

A Glass Of Orange Juice

I need it in the morning
a part of simple living
the sun still yawning
but all her light she is giving

I knew the only way through
was to find happiness in everything
when the sky wasn't blue
but it still felt like spring

Making fresh orange juice
pouring it into a glass kilner jar
aesthetically would give me a boost
enough vitamin C to take me far

I knew in your final days it gave you relief
when eating was a task in itself
sometimes that orange juice is all you need
even when ill, to bring you health

A conversation we shared
we said orange juice felt like liquid gold
sometimes nothing can compare
especially when the glass is freezing cold

We both lived gently
enjoyed the small pleasures in life
a glass of orange juice was plenty
the only way to start the day right

Lost In The Wind

It's been a month since the wind took you
I didn't even have chance to breathe
if I knew which direction the wind blew
maybe I'd have a chance to grieve

With one gust you were gone
it blew me off my feet
I landed somewhere I didn't belong
I couldn't even speak

Now I must find my way back
the road seems long and confusing
I must not go off track
the wind is all consuming

Pink Lady

I can't look at pictures without feeling thirteen again
my heart aching for that girl unaware of how fast time dissipates
not like a rotten apple degrading slowly
returning to the soil where she was first born
a Pink Lady
selfless, full of goodness, needed everyday
but lightening flashes too fast to absorb
blind-sided by the velocity
I want to reach into the photo and pull you out
stuck in a place I want to revisit
Lyme Regis beach, 99 with a flake
the Blue Volvo spluttering up the hill
past children who didn't see it's character
not even me
before my feet even touched the ground
before I knew you
twenty four short years together, fifty more without you
a fraction of time too small to even hold
but I would live in it forever
if it meant we were together

Not Your Home

What he took from me I can't get back
he said I was where he laid his hat

I wanted to be more than where he took off his clothes
a comfy sofa with lime throws

A home I built with my own hands
crafted upon the golden sands

But I walked barefoot, no shoes
burnt soles, feet all bruised

An open fire toasting marshmallows
under the flame, skin orange-yellow

Laying naked as they all stare
embers of my clothes flying through the air

To Be Found

I was lost waiting to be found
like a stolen IKEA pencil wedged between a car seat
writing poetry on food receipts
love notes over last weeks shopping list
the one pound in your bag on the hottest day in June
a volvic to quench your thirst
not satisfying enough but ten pound short for a Naked Smoothie
a hairband on your gear stick
windswept in your green Beatle
singing to The 1975 until you can't breathe
I wanted to be found by someone in need
in my time of need, they all fell short
a siren just echoing back, self inflicted headache
I had to force feed myself ginger biscuits so I wasn't sick
eating bread to soak up the anguish
instead of being surrounded by friends who made me feel invincible
skin to skin we can take on anything
they weren't there
instead I spoke to the waves
I found solace in feeling small
I floated like a buoy near the beach front
my last purpose
to stop others from drowning to

The Tea Tree

Everything I have is my own
a water colour kit is all I needed
I painted with my tears alone
to make a picture, I need to feel it

Everything I have I created
I sit back and wonder where it call came from
I got out my brush, with love I made it
to make a painting, I let the feelings come

It was me who made it happen
I stopped the world and created my own
finger to A4, soft like satin
painting the trees that I have grown

Too many tears caused ripples in the paper
diluted the brightness of the colours
to my painting this was a saviour
as waves ripple to greet one another

A spilt cup of Yorkshire, I dropped my tea
on the canvas of so many different textures
with the brown stain, I painted my tree
finding beauty in the misadventures

White Flag

I drew my white flag in chalk
I knew it could wipe off if needs be
I drew it where people would walk
it needed to be where people would see

I thought I wouldn't surrender for long
soon I would be right back
wondering if this is where I belong
or if fear of the unknown kept me on track

With a moment of rain my flag would disappear
then I could decide whether it was worth being alone
before I surrender to all of my fears
walking away all on my own

We as women have strength
we just think too much with our hearts
I saw his red flag all ripped on the ends
but thought I could mend the broken parts

I sewed it and painted it
after it got broken in the storm
I loved and rearranged it
trying to reveal its true form

If thinking with our heart is our biggest downfall
then that's one I'm going to be proud of
when faced with such hate in this world
I can't be ashamed to love

The rain came but the white flag stayed
Mother teaching me a lesson
it's better to be alone than unhappy, always
our open hearts, our biggest blessing

Forever In The Sycamore

I've been wondering when the trees last saw us
they watched us grow together
it should've been the other way around
but there were changes in the weather

In the moment we always stayed
walking with the towering sycamore
love was always handmade
I will tell them you're not sick anymore

My last visit to the blue river
feet deep in the folding waters
for Mother Nature to deliver
she must have saw us as her daughters

She grew the material we used as shoes
protected by the resilient vines
lessons I will always use
to stay within the lines

A camouflage frame
but also the most telling
I'll carve your name
so they'll never forget the spelling

Strawberry Summer

Have you ever been kissed by the sun
and kissed by her
it's almost too much to handle
in the light of strawberry summer
she radiates warmth

Almost too sweet to touch
almost too perfect to kiss
bright red but never embarrassed
confident in her skin

Two hundred perfect seeds
preserved for those willing to wait
there is no rush in strawberry summer
everything is at her pace

A perfect shape
one taste and I am hooked
sun kissed in summer
whilst my lips she also took

Into The Flames

I lit my fire with a gas lighter
it was meant to warm me up, but it just burnt me
that's the last time I rely on something else
I should've ran
to get the blood flowing
I should've put on my pink jumper
instead of being exposed and vulnerable
I should've hugged myself for comfort
instead of finding warmth in someone else's arms
I should've walked from the fire
and not fallen

Empty Vase

I'm told what is mine won't escape me
but they just keep getting away
I heard today isn't promised
to live like it's my last day
but Monday he left me
and Tuesday felt so grey
I'll see my friends on Saturday
to shake some pain away
I'll tattoo "if he wanted to he would"
on my forehead, to not see but remember
what is mine won't escape me
it's gonna be a long December
I told him I like yellow sunflowers
he passes the shop everyday
but the vase has stayed empty
maybe another day

Don't Be Scared Of The Spider

Trying to free myself from this web
sharing a home with a dead fly
covers still unmade on my bed
I haven't showered since the last time I cried

I can only thank him for tangling me between two branches
at least I can sit and watch the day go by
waiting for someone to come and take their chances
wondering what facing their fears would feel like

Two weeks of unshaven legs
skin like cactus prickles
I still haven't managed to break the silver threads
much stronger than they are fickle

I held a spider in my primary school playground
I had to break his home to reach it
curiosity always seems to find its way back round
it was a lot less frightening to feel it

My teacher told me "don't be scared of the spider, you might be
helping someone get free"
when I was young and naïve
now I wonder if someone will do that for me
and break through this home, in curiosity

Silent Lovers

A girl sat behind you on the train whilst fifty bodies moved but stayed still, personifying how she felt, she was moved by your music choice, but she didn't tell you. She thought you were tender, the train glided as the lights flickered between platforms, like you were backstage at a concert, you were the main character in her tale. She told her friends of the girl in purple, listening to her favourite artist.

A girl walked past you in Costa whilst you ordered a mango cooler, a brave choice to go to a coffee shop and not order coffee, she was intrigued. She Googled "red top with yellow flowers" after she saw you in yours, too shy to ask, but she thought you were beautiful.

A girl watched you shelter from the rain under a conifer tree, it started raining needles on your hair, wet but also covered in foliage, you took it in your stride. Courageous to be out in a storm but dogs still need walking, selfless. Hair soaking wet, she wondered how someone could still look so radiant.

These are your silent lovers, you possess something admired by each person. They all fell for you in peace, *the greatest kind of love.*

Home Bird

Birthed by the water
first moments in the white bathroom sink
a raisin waiting to be ironed out by Mother, never Father
my first time flying when he put his feet on my torso
lifted me to the ceiling
I could free myself but when the fire was lit
the table was laid
food was prepared
I didn't need to
worms cut into little pieces
hand fed to me so I didn't choke

I knew of many birds
birthed indoors to now be chased away by little feet
vermin to mankind
my first time outdoors I saluted a magpie
like I had always been told
he looked at me bewildered
he didn't know the power he held
it was safer to be a home bird
I was too sheltered to fly with my kin
I knew too much

Colours That Make Me Feel Safe

A lavender bath with a lush bath bomb
a picnic blanket in a green meadow
a pink haze after the sun has gone
my brown teddy I won't ever outgrow

My favourite blue Levi's jeans
my fluffy ginger kitten
some buttery toast with orange beans
black lines where my poetry is handwritten

The red gryffindor common room
seeing the end of a rainbow
a Yorkshire tea stirred with a silver spoon
a birthday chocolate gateau

Stone cottages in little towns
homemade tomato soup with seasoning
my lilac converse that cost me too many pounds
gold fairy lights on a winter evening

Soul Searching

The journey to the soul is one like no other
once found, you must protect her like a mother

Feed, nurture, listen, just know you will be tired
so much strength inside is required

You will watch her make mistakes, she will be defiant
but after everything, on you she is reliant

Boys will hurt her, you must let her heart take shape
mould itself around every mistake

Friends will come and go, some days she will feel alone
as long as she knows, the safest place is her home

This is where her earliest memories will form
she will carry them with her, through every storm

Until the last venture, where the soul is ready
you've given it enough room to flourish, steadily

She's seen every colour, not one she prefers
for the soul to evolve, the spectrum must be diverse

Intimacy

Kiss my shoulders gently
where I carry the weight of the world
a colony on my collarbones
rosy lips to mottled skin
one finger down the bridge of my nose
where many wouldn't cross
interlocked fingers
as if we were building our own walkway
untangle my hairs from one another
even if they want to be close
warm water tickling cold skin
cream to soften the sharp edges
cradle my stomach
to calm the earthquakes
to ready the home I will harbour life
be gentle with my backbone
it's still growing slowly
feel my feet
ridges imprinted on my soles
from barefoot wanders
ready my journey
with gentleness

Tainted Waters

I wanted to be held, not held back
he looked me in my eyes
brown meeting blue for the first time
the way it merged wasn't what you'd expect
a muddy lake touching a lucent stream
the way it joined together, an oxymoron
it was a known secret that opposites didn't attract
those echos of how we wouldn't work
after I handed you my personality and let you run with it
a current I couldn't follow
blinded by mire, you tainted my sheer body
until more of me was dark
and all of you was pure

Feel Like Summer

To heal is to feel
then let go of the sorrow
the feelings aren't real
they'll be diluted tomorrow

The past has now passed
have faith in your pace
you made it here at last
even if you weren't in the race

Slow doesn't mean you won't grow
to blossom it must be forgotten
you can face it and then let it go
leave it, it will go rotten

Your plight is your fight
your colour is not duller
it doesn't have to be bright
for it to feel like summer

Passing Pictures

If I could tell my life in pictures - what would I paint?
I wouldn't need to think of the right words to say
practice my vocabulary - no awkward silences
strangers I meet, people I pass day by day
I'll make six pictures for those who matter
pass them on without conversation
a self portrait for my mum
for teaching me I am enough
a croissant for my boyfriend
a breakfast made with love
a golden sunset for my nan and grandad
they are always there
a wardrobe for my sister
for all the clothes that we share
a cup of tea for my best friend
there is nothing more I need
a tree to remind myself
that even when lost
I can breathe

Grief In Life

It wasn't just the day you were gone
it was the day your house sold
the smell of bubbling cheese on potato
fresh onions from your allotment
a homemade stew
just knowing grandad was there
his curly hair poking above the chair
I had to leave my childhood that day

It was the day I heard Johnny Mathis
dancing in mums kitchen
a slice of strawberry sponge
to hear you sing one more time
music to my ears

It will be Christmas Day
an empty seat and a glass of shloer
I will still wrap up your presents
two packs of flamed raisins
a tin of roses

It will be everyday
for the rest of my life
until I cook my grandchildren stew
tell them all about you

Waking At Sunset

My parents told me I missed the whole day
that I fell asleep at sunrise
I told them it's the best way
if you really want to open your eyes

I woke to splashes of pink
pools of orange underneath
it really made me think
the silence will let me breathe

The moon was waiting with an iced coffee
we meet just after sunset
the very moment the orange leaves softly
I jump right out of bed

Something about stillness outside
makes me feel less alone
nothing else left to decide
comfy in my home

Moving Time

I've done 24 circles round the sun
I tried to stop feeling dizzy
even though the journeys just begun
I still feel like the years will miss me

290 circles around me
a second to take it all in
just enough time to see
my story finally begin

Sea Of Green

A sea of green
places I've never been
even if I don't feel like it
it is all that I need

The way it stretches
is never reckless
perfecly crafted
almost breathless

Between the trees
thirty two degrees
a sea of green
the only time I can breathe

Between the flow
I feel protected
forced in a current
a new perspective

Floating towards resistance
going against my instincts
realising this journey
isn't about distance

Something In The Water

Call me old fashioned
put on a black and white movie
I don't want to see anything other than two lovers dancing
four synchronised feet in black shoes
this new love is low
sitting somewhere in the Mariana Trench
beside creatures undiscovered
they don't know how to love
only survive
they act on instincts
it must be something in the water

I want it to rain on me
just to see if he will open the umbrella
ache his arms for my shelter
call me old fashioned
but I don't want to wear this new love
eyes like torches in the sweet shop
a bucket full of pic n mix
fizzy cola bottles or strawberry laces
I'll have both
drowning in choice
it must be something in the water

Comfort Blanket

I knitted you when I was lonely
you were cold too but never showed me
my patchwork pretender
full of holes but could always mend her
until the winter wasn't kind
burying every nut I could find
I needed energy after giving mine away
you grew stronger by the day
fog on my glasses
I couldn't see past this
you were my comfort blanket
I helped make you but you couldn't stand it
you were pink and I was blue
I was old and you were new
one acorn a day was enough for me to see
this blanket was only temporary

Head 2 Head

I'm head to head with myself
just two sad brains
always fighting
like a married couple that are trying to stay together for the kids
I know we need to divorce
so I can move somewhere
more peaceful

I want to love my brain like I love my best friend
purely platonic
we spend time together because we want to
not because we are trying to mend a broken family
we laugh and sing and dance
until we are red in the face
we have freedom to express ourselves
my safe space

I think in order to find peace I must divorce my brain
then love myself like a best friend
a best friend I became

Grey Area

It's where I go to think
a place isolated with memories
I pick one out the kitchen sink
to show me what I couldn't see

My childhood bedroom
a box shaped souvenir
it won't fit in my head soon
it's too cluttered in here

My first kiss in bed
where he took it all from me
somewhere to lay my head
to sleep so I can't see

The sun didn't shine through after that
although I left the window open
the last bit of light was where I sat
through the grey, my soul was woven

Mothers Love

I don't know when the transition comes
from a Mother to a best friend
one day it just clicks, like the seatbelt you protected me with
it clicks like the fingers you wiped my tears with
always side by side but not always close
now together we're bound, from years of turbulence
to look at you and realise we're infact the same
I didn't argue with you because I didn't love you
I argued because you loved me too much
it wasn't as welcomed as it is now
too many colours I couldn't see
I guess that's on being young
it's hard to understand feelings that you've never felt
I still don't fully understand but some colours are clear
a mothers love is never one to fear

Simplicity

I wouldn't call myself a poet
just a girl wanting to hear beautiful things
sweet words dripping off the tongue
like honey in the mouth of a badger
if I lived with animals I think we'd have a simple life
at least predators make themselves known
the sun calls me up at dawn
I've got nowhere to be
a fox caught in daylight
not something you always see

To The Core

I peeled back my layers
like ripping off a plaster
only the underneath hadn't healed yet
I knew she was somewhere deep down
I just needed to find her
one soft call and she was ready
each one I peeled back
a memory shed
leading me to the core
it was stronger than I last remembered
a pink beacon
supporting me whilst I supported her
exposed and vulnerable, we needed new skin
layers of memories to make
where we were finally in love

Sun Birth

I set myself on fire
for so long I have lived in the shade
I burned from the inside out
to show them how far I came
I put a mirror to the orange sun
watched my skin take shape
she is watching me finally become
the woman that she raised

Aries Moon

They say life moves in phases
like the moon and its faces
I've never looked up to the Aries moon
I think it'll leave me soon
at the first quarter I'll reminisce
for all the colour that I've missed
I asked the moon to show me what I couldn't see
there are things you can't find in astrology
he told me there is more to life if you grab it
I told him that I'm a creature of habit
there is strength in leaving the one
but I need to stay until I know it's done
I can't have any regrets
the full moon is all I have left

Your Garden

I told him the grass is only greener where you water it
if it's not nourished, how do you expect it to grow
he said if we only loved one type of plant
why do we put so many on show
I told him to enjoy plants
is like enjoying the music
without having to dance

Whole

I want to be loved so deep
it swallows me whole
lying comfy on the tongue
where I leave them speechless
my pink mattress
lubricate my body
so I slide down the throat
into the belly
where I am born again
but this time
whole

Love Like Them

I never thought I was clingy
until I was told by my past lovers
even if love ends up stinging me
like the bee trapped under my covers

I love in abundance
I give it my all
even if it becomes redundant
it's what will catch me when I fall

My red tartan blanket
to capture my tired body
they just can't handle it
love isn't a hobby

Flying Colours

All the things I've done
all the things I've seen
all my teenage years spent sleeping in the clouds
nothing matters when you're with friends everyday
all those nights I felt worthy
each inch of my body craved
I wasn't fully developed but I was happy feeling small
a delicate bird, underfed but you felt drawn to it
you'd rescue it from the road but you can't touch it
then I flew with broken wings all the way to my twenties
I passed so many colours on the way
I never stopped to take them all in
the viridescent blades of glass
they carved stories into my tissue
now scars of my past
sometimes I touch them to revisit
I would go back if I could

Leaving Me

Half of me I wanted to lose
my want for attention
my lack of boundaries
the embedded self doubt
the voices of reason I argued with
indecisiveness
the replay of every conversation I've ever had
a bad movie directed by myself
the other half I tried so hard to keep
I fought the anxiety, but I was unprepared
parts of me lost on the battlefield
I lost my soul when my grandparents died
I tried to hold on to the dust
but they took it with them to the other side
I gave myself to too many people
parts of me handed out willingly
I thought selflessness would rebuild me
half of me given, half of me taken

Finding Her

I found her naked in the sand
she managed to grow a single flower in the drought
villagers flocked to see the beauty
a newly discovered shade of purple
a lavender gift
her roots stretched under the ground
the flower was still yet supple
she welcomed life to desolate land
a lotis blue on her petal
a royal beauty
to dig herself up would cause destruction
but to stay, was to outgrow
she knew that to move her flower
to spread her seeds
would cause temporary disappointment
but in the long run
a lifetime of beauty
she left the villagers bare
feet on stark land once again
but in fifty years a sea of flowers
one colour at a time
the patience of a saint

Colours That Make Me Feel Alive

Red face and nose after a cold walk
grey moon reflecting on the sea at night
black coffee over a morning talk
white city lights from up high

Pink confetti falling after my favourite song at a concert
gold glitter on my face at a festival
twirling around in a floaty white skirt
a strawberry ice cream on a hot day is plentiful

Yellow flowers painted on a white canvas
silver stars that are one billion years old
the red blood moon guiding me as she dances
a charity shop brown mug that hasn't yet been sold

A purple blueberry smoothie for breakfast
sipping a lemon Fanta on holiday
a midnight cinema trip for a pink tango ice blast
listening to Channel Orange on the motorway

I Want To Feel

I want to feel
I want to feel everything
I want to feel suffocated by the wind
I want to feel my heart break
I want to feel it slowly heal
I want to feel alive in the rain
I want to feel alone in this world
I want to feel like I belong here
I want to feel loved, deeply
I want to feel needed, solely
I want to feel lost
I want to feel the sun
I want to feel her colours
I want to feel laughter in my belly
I want to feel each tear stain my face
I want to feel the wind change as I smile
I want to feel it all
just for a little while

Growing And Glowing

I've poured my soul into this book and now I'm ready to find another
I've loved so much and now I'm ready to find a lover
I always feel like I should give more than what you can see
how can I give more without losing parts of me
my skin was pale like an overcast sky
the January blues always come by
I put it down to lack of iron in my diet
or maybe that my brain wouldn't stay quiet
but each day flushed the pink out my cheeks
each blue winter left me weak at the knees
up to my ears in spinach and broccoli
chasing the colour hoping someone would follow me
it lead me to myself, forced me to climb within
to seek the hidden light, the glow in my skin

The Way It Goes

I thought I'd be married by 25
not just trying to get by

When I got here I realised I was out of my depth
learning everything I didn't know yet

It's hard to learn and heal simultaneously
I end up just wandering aimlessly

Procrastinate so I don't get overwhelmed
hard to plan the future when the past still needs to mend

Now I realise what's more important than saying I do
the white gown that I can see right through

Is wanting to spend the rest of my life with myself
before I try to love anybody else

I was told I look happy today,
I wondered what made him think that. The red
glow in my cheeks, my bright white eyes, the dark
circles had diminished now I was able to sleep. My
hair, a rich shade of auburn, growing from the
nutrients swimming through my body. I was
healing and it was obvious, I couldn't hide it any
longer. The colour inside me was restored through
self love. My beauty was happiness, a compliment
like music to my ears, the kind of song that sends
goosebumps up your arms. I opened them and
welcomed myself back, I can't wait to show her
what she's missed.

Printed in Great Britain
by Amazon